House Cleaning Made Easy

How To Clean Your House Fast, Easy And Clutter Free

Table of Contents

Introduction

A man's own house is their own palace, so they say. After a long and tiresome day, all one needs is to get back to their house, apartment or condominium and rest. However, there is more to it than just sleeping. The cleanliness of your house will have a profound effect on whether you will actually enjoy the much-needed rest after a long day's work. A clean house is not only good for your health; it is also good for making you attain your desired peace of mind. A clean house provides some kind of sense of security. It is of essence to note that a clean self and a clean home will also enhance your mood and raise your spirit. So, if you have been taking the general cleanliness of your house less seriously, you should start putting it in check. In as much as everyone knows that keeping the house clean should be an everyday activity, most of us end up accumulating lots of clutter such that our houses become messy and uncomfortable places to live in. You may even get to a point of being afraid of coming home or visiting certain rooms because of the big mess that has accumulated for weeks, months or even years. Truth be told, most of us would do anything to undo that. The only problem is that you cannot maintain this unless you know how to actually clean the house and keep it clean.

Dirt hides in some of the most unexpected places in the house. This book will help you discover where exactly not to ignore when it comes to cleaning the house. As you get started on this, your #1 strategy should be to divide and conquer. In simple terms, view each room or section of the house one at a time and not as one whole mess of dirt. Divide your house into zones and everyday clean every zone for at least five minutes. As you begin your house cleaning work, it is advisable to play your favorite jam on your stereo, as this can be a good mood booster. You will be amazed by how fast and easy you will clean different rooms without actually noticing whether 10 minutes or more have passed. Let's get started in the actual cleaning process.

The Kitchen

De-Cluttering And Cleaning The Kitchen

Before you start doing any cleaning work on any part of the kitchen, it is important to do some quick de-cluttering first. This should make it easier to clean various parts of the kitchen. Pick up anything that is in the kitchen that should not be there; it could be your wallet or handbag, watch or some clothes that you forgot in the kitchen for one reason or another. As you do so, you should classify everything you pick up into either clutter for disposal, clutter to give out or items to keep but move to a different part of the house. Here is how you can actually clean different parts of the kitchen. Even as you clean the different parts, start by de-cluttering and using the same classification technique for different forms of clutter.

Stove

The stove is the center of your kitchen. So, do not be surprised to learn that it can be the dirtiest of them all. This is because of grease and food droppings that gather around it as time goes by forming a whole lot of dirt strips. In cleaning the stove, soak drip pans and knobs in warm soapy water and work around it cleaning all the sides before doing the final wiping using an old dry towel to give it some shine. Remove pans from the top of the stoves once you are done with the cooking and keep them in the kitchen cabinets after washing to lessen the clutter.

The sink

It is said that the sink has more bacteria than the toilet seat. The next time a plumber gets your broken sink done, if you get a chance to look inside the pipes that drain water to the drainage, you will quite agree that it can get pretty dirty than you think. To disinfect your sink, clean your sink using soapy water, then use vinegar to spray all round and if you have hydrogen peroxide, you can use it instead. Mineral oil can be used to do the final buffing to give your sink a final sparkling shine. You should always restrain from letting dirty dishes overstay in the sink to avoid the clutter and eyesore of dirty dishes piling up in the sink. The simple trick is to wash the dishes as soon as possible.

The cutting boards

Chopping boards can get smelly if not cleaned regularly. Wash cutting boards with liquid dishwashing detergent and water to keep them clean. Soak in a solution of regular bleach such as Clorox Regular bleach and let the boards stand for three minutes then let them dry. Rubbing halved lemons onto the cutting boards can also assist in reducing odors. This should be concluded by rinsing with cold water.

Wash your dishwasher

Your dishwasher is the one that takes care of your previous nights' remains of that great dinner you had with a couple of friends. It is important to clean it thoroughly so that it remains in top condition. For at least once every week, wash your dishwasher by using baking soda on a damp sponge and wiping it around the machine's edge to get rid of stuck food stains. Also, remember to clean the inside by running an empty cycle with any product designed to kill bacteria.

The refrigerator

Your refrigerator can be a total mess when it comes to cleanliness but no matter how gross it may be, there is always a way of going about it. It is good to keep things that go bad quickly where you can spot them lest you find them badly stuck to your refrigerator. Rotting veggies, bad meat, and stuff like that should be placed at the front of the refrigerator compartments so that it does not get you off-guard the next time you open your refrigerator. Clean the edge of your fridge, as many people do not even think of the gunk that collects there. Use a touch of hot water and vinegar to clean repeatedly. Many people mostly forget the top of the fridge, as it does not come to mind quite often. In many homes, this site is usually left to collect dust and other stuff that may get their way their only to be forgotten completely. Using a spray cleaner, a box and paper towels, start by removing everything placed on top of the fridge and place them in a box. Spray the cleaner over the top of the fridge then wipe the dust and dirt using a paper towel until clean.

Garbage disposal

In most occasions, we throw fruit peels, shells, and rotten stuff down the drain. You need to remember that the disposal should be used to dispose off only biodegradable trash such as vegetables and fruit peels. Run a few cups of ice cubes through the disposal to help sharpen the blades to improve the grinding power.

Mask odors in your trashcans by placing a couple of dryer sheets in the bottom. Place extra garbage bags at the bottom of the trash can and take out trash.

To disinfect the trashcan, simply spray a cleaner with bleach until thoroughly wet.

Clean the whole kitchen

Keeping the kitchen tidy is a process. So once you have had different items cleaned, it is time to clean the visible surfaces including the kitchen floor, the cupboards and various other parts that could be accumulating dirt.

Once you have cleaned the whole kitchen, it is time to organize. Below are some amazing organization ideas that you can try especially if you don't have such a large kitchen.

Kitchen Organization Ideas

If you live in a small apartment with a small kitchen, there are plenty of ways you can make it look organized. Here are a few tips and tricks you can use to make the most of the limited room:

*Pot lid storage

Have a towel bar installed above your stove for storing pot lids. Whenever you remove the lid from a pot, you can store it in the towel bar, instead of setting down on the counter space.

*Make use of the space above your doorway

If you are like any other family, chances are that you do not use the space above your doorway, so you can hang a shelf there. If you don't have space to put your liquor cabinet, you can convert part of a pallet to a shelf to accommodate a couple of bottles, and then mount it above your doorway. If you are not tall enough to get to the shelf without using a step stool, be sure not to store things that you are going to need every few minutes.

Store measuring spoons in a jar

Sometimes it can be quite frustrating when you are trying to find a measuring spoon in a drawer and you cannot simply find it. A great way of ensuring that your measuring spoons are not hard to find is storing them in the jar by the stove. Not only does this make it easy to find the spoons but it also keeps the drawers neat by not having the spoons all over.

*Create cheerful and open storage

Open up your kitchen by removing the upper cabinet doors. The open shelving will make the room feel bigger. You can also stick wallpapers on the insides of the cabinets to add a pop of color

*If you are short on cabinet space, store items on your counters

If your kitchen does not have plenty of cabinet space, you can place the items you use frequently at the top of your counters. However, be sure to keep everything organized so that you can reach it easily whenever you need it. Additionally, be sure to reserve the front half for preparing food.

*Use trays to organize items on your counters

For instance, if you make tea most days, you can keep all your beverage making items and tea on a tray, right beside your stove so that you don't have to run all over the kitchen when looking for something.

*Use labels to keep things organized

Labeling the containers is the easiest way to keep anything organized. Doing this not only makes storing things efficient, but it also makes it easy to find them when you are looking for them. When labeling containers, make sure that the labels are visible once you store the containers. Place labels over anything you are storing in a drawer or over the counters, and at the front of anything going into a cabinet.

*Store your favorite recipes in a close binder

You can place your recipe binder on the counter, and fill it with all your favorite recipes. Whenever you find a great recipe, you can just type it, print it, and then stick it in the binder. Tab dividers can make it very easy to find what you are looking for, and you can pull out one page at a time, and then leave it on the counter for reference. If anything spills, you can just wipe it up using a sponge.

*Hang things up instead of storing them over the counter or inside a drawer

Hang your hot pads on a 3m hook on the exterior of your upper cabinets. This way, they can become easily accessible, and they won't take up much space in your drawers. Additionally, the 3m hooks are efficient in that they won't cause permanent damage to your cabinets when you extract them. Paper towels are another thing you can hang. You can mount a paper towel holder under an upper cabinet to free up counter space.

*Get a portable dishwasher

If you don't already own a dishwasher, you can purchase a portable one. Portable dishwashers are usually designed with casters, so you can roll them away when not in use. On the other hand, if your kitchen is spacious enough to accommodate it, you can place it near the sink and utilize the top for additional counter space.

*Use a magnetic knife rack to store your knives

It is very easy to install magnetic knife racks, and they are incredibly handy. They keep knives readily accessible so you don't have to search all over the kitchen, or give up counter space to store the knives.

*Keep useful items within easy reach

When it comes to keeping your counters reasonably clear, there is one time when this rule is not true, as far as the kitchen sink is concerned. You definitely want to keep essential dish cleaning supplies on the counter in order to avoid opening a cabinet or drawer with wet and soapy hands to find a brush or sponge.

But you don't have to place everything on the counter. You can install a bar right above the sink where you can hang a drying dishcloth. If you are a garden enthusiast, you can hang your watering can immediately above your sink using a small picture hanger. It is perfect in that it is not taking up any counter space, and you can reach it whenever you want to water your plants.

*Make use of the back of cabinet doors

Invest in a good organizer to hang over a cabinet door for storing cleaning supplies. These are excellent because they come with a rod that hangs on the outside besides the organizers that are in the cabinet. This is great for hanging dishtowels.

You can also get a magnetic spice rack to hang on the inner side of cabinet doors just to ensure that the spices do not take up any space on the pantry shelves, they are easy to find, and you can see exactly how much spice is left.

*Use the ceiling to hang produce

Install a hanging basket from the ceiling to store your produce and keep it organized and off the counter.

*Create a drop space in the entrance

If your house has a backdoor that leads to the kitchen, you can create a drop space for your sunglasses and keys so that they don't end up on the counters.

*It is not necessary to use your dine-in area if you don't want to

If your dining table can fit in another room, you can use the space in your dine-in kitchen for extra storage. You can put a desk and use it as a command center, or add open shelving for pantry. Keep in mind that your kitchen is your own space and you can organize it the way you want. Just get creative!

The Washrooms

De-Cluttering The Bathroom

The bathroom as well needs to be de-cluttered to give ample space to anyone who may want to use it. This is because most bathrooms have limited space because of their compact nature. As already mentioned, remove anything that doesn't belong in the washroom and place it in its rightful place; it could be in the trash can, the giveaway bin or the transfer to another room basket. Use the basket to stash any empty cans, dirty towels and other unwanted items to be sorted out later after you are done with the bathroom in a bid to keep your movements minimal.

Also, try to put the like items together to avoid getting everything mixed up and giving you problems later on. You can sort stuff into different categories such as cosmetics, hair accessories, shaving items and nail care items. If you share the bathroom with other people, it will be prudent to designate a shelf, a basket, a drawer and such like to each person to avoid having everything everywhere and actually losing some stuff in the clutter. For instance, you could separate mens' drawers from women's drawers.

Cleaning The Bathroom
Cleaning the surfaces

The washroom is one sensitive area in your house in that you simply cannot avoid it and its condition determines whether life in your house will be comfortable. Clean the sinks, the mirror, and the other surfaces using disinfectant. It is good to wet the stains in advance as you carry on with other cleaning activities around the washrooms for ease of removal. Remember to remove toothpaste splashes on the floors and walls, as these make the place look ugly. Remove anything that doesn't belong in the washroom and place it where it belongs; you should use the strategy mentioned in kitchen cleaning by classifying clutter into giveaway, trash and keep or transfer to another area. Anything that does not belong in the washroom should be kept away in its appropriate place. It is better to move around with a basket as you clean to stuff anything that needs to be moved. Also, have a trashcan in place to stuff all the trash and to avoid too many movements and maximize the effectiveness of every move. The idea is simple; moving wastes seconds and each second wasted doing nothing constructive translates to wasting more time cleaning and organizing your house.

Scrub the bathroom floor with a hard brush and detergent to remove accumulated dirt and grease. Clean the doorknobs with a disinfectant as these carry a whole lot of germs because of being handled with dirty hands every time. Clean the toilet thoroughly using a disinfectant and then spray an air freshener to give the washrooms that fresh welcoming scent. You can also opt for scented candles instead of the air freshener. Remember to buy washroom supplies, as you don't want to run out of this at the time you need them most. Wash and replace any dirty towels that could be hanging around the bathroom. In cleaning your shower curtain, use about one cup of vinegar and bleach. Adding a fabric softener will help in cleaning the curtain. When you are done with the washing, put back the curtains back to dry.

Cleaning the water tub

Use body wash or liquid shower gel in your tub and not ordinary soap as that will minimize any chances of scum building up on the surface of the tub. You can also use a disinfecting bathroom cleaner to remove any scum that is already built up and there is no scrubbing required in doing this.

Wipe bathtubs with a product that can be used to kill moulds. This will ensure mildew or mold do not grow. The same product can be used to clean glazed ceramic tiles. Just spray the surface with the disinfecting bathroom Cleaner, (Clorox is mostly preferable) and let the product stand for at least half an hour before wiping.

Remove any excess items on the ledge of your tub and try to get something that can help you sort things better.

Cleaning the toothbrush

We use our toothbrush to remove all the germs from our mouth each day, so it's no wonder it gets a little nasty itself. However, it isn't unheard of to find ourselves failing to clean the toothbrush to remove/kill any accumulated germs. So, how do you go about cleaning the toothbrush to keep it germ free? Start by ensuring that you run hot water daily through your toothbrush bristles and using pressure when you rub the bristles while running the water. Daily use of your toothbrush can also be a form of cleaning it so it is advisable to use one toothbrush before deciding to replace instead of swapping multiple ones on different days. Soaking your toothbrush in mouthwash for about a minute is recommended as also a good way of disinfecting your toothbrush. Another good way to disinfect your toothbrush is by boiling it in hot water for some minutes to kill germs. As you do all that, ensure that you wash your hands before handling your toothbrush, as that will reduce the amount of germ spread that may occur. All this will reduce the germs and bacteria that may live in your toothbrush.

Bathroom Organization Tips

Have you ever noticed how stuff tends to accumulate in the bathroom? Sure, you need quite a few products for your beauty routines, but that does not mean you have to live in a messy space. Here are a few organizational tips for your bathroom.

*Pitch it

Before starting, ensure that there are no extraneous items lying around that need to be trashed, but not put away. Watch if the medications and vitamins in your medicine cabinet have expired, and trash the expired sunscreen as well. Additionally, keep tabs on the length of time you have had your makeup. Different products have different shelf lives. This is not the time to get sentimental about any of your beauty products. As a general rule of thumb, if you are not using it, trash it. This way, you will create more space for new products.

*How is it hanging?

Instead of piling your magazines at the back of the toilet sink, install a magazine rack on one side of the wall where you can store them. Look for a place that will not eat up too much bathroom space, and one that is out of the way. On the other hand, ensure that the storage space is convenient for the user.

*Divide and conquer

Install utensil organizers in drawers that have cotton swabs, safety pins, bobby pins, elastic hair bands, and so on. This will ensure that everything has its own storage space, and that you can be able to reach what you want when you need it.

*Sample not

Do you have the habit of holding onto small bottles of conditioner and shampoo, and tiny soaps from hotels you have frequented? Have you ever used these products or are you simply saving them for a rainy day? Chances are you won't need them when travelling, since there will be more soaps and bottles of conditioner and shampoo; therefore, get rid of them.

*Contain the clutter

Use a mesh bag to store your kid's bath toys, where they can be able to drain and dry when not in use. Let your kids learn to clean up the bathroom every time they bathe. For shave gels, body washes, conditioners, and shampoos, find a caddy that can stick to the wall, hangs from the shower faucet, or attaches in a corner.

*Cabinet revamp

If you are like most people, chances are you tend to throw everything in the cabinet under your bathroom sink, and forget about it. Take inventory, and once more, trash what you don't need, including empty cleaning supplies and old scour pads. Invest in another caddy with a handle, for storing cleaning products in order to move it easily when cleaning from bathroom to bathroom.

*Ribbon renewal

You can organize your daughter's hair clips, and display them at the same time. Besides, those cute bows are so attractive that you can still show them off even when she is not wearing them on her hair. Hang a nice ribbon on the wall and store all the clips there.

*Clean constantly

Rather than waiting for your bathroom to become cluttered before you can clean it, consider tidying it up a little bit every day. In the end, this little step will save you plenty of time. Store disinfectant wipes in the caddy under the counter, where you can easily reach them when wiping the counters after putting everything away.

*Cord less

Try investing in hairstyling accessories such as straight irons, hot curlers, and blow dryers that have retractable cords. Otherwise, ensure that you always wrap up the cords neatly after you are done with the equipment, but remember to wait for it to cool first.

*Handy towels

Install a standalone rack or shelf above the toilet for additional storage space. You can use this to store a few extra hand towels, simple decorations, or fancy guest soaps.

*Organize your medicine cabinet

Your medicine cabinet should be a repository of the things you need and use frequently. This means you have to remove any outdated medicines and relocate the excess to another location. Your medicine cabinet is best used for daily grooming, as opposed to medicines.

Store like items together in labeled storage bins in the linen closet or underneath the sink. Whenever you need something, you can simply slide out the whole container for easy access. Medicines are better stored in the kitchen, since moisture can ruin them. When you create active storage space in your medicine cabinet, you can minimize the time you spend in the bathroom.

*Divide your makeup

Most people tend to drop all kinds of containers in dividers in the bathroom, most of which are badly organized. You can also set up an expandable drawer organizer for the cosmetics. This is designed to fit in a shallow drawer and will often replace the pretty heavy cosmetic bags that you have probably been keeping. You can use compartments that are of different sizes just to help you organize the eye shadow, blush, and lipstick so you never have to ransack the whole bathroom when looking for something. When organizing your makeup, remember to throw away anything that is expired or smells. Old makeup is riddled with bacteria that can cause skin irritation.

*Reassess your shower caddy

It might be your best friend when in the shower, but is it ideal for you? Shower caddies that are either too large or too small can be a pain, both when cleaning your shower, and when bathing. There are several alternatives, including corner caddies, suction shelves, and over the showerhead. You can always pare down your toiletries if you don't have enough space.

*Use apothecary jars to add style and function

If there's plenty of counter space in your bathroom, and you don't mind leaving things out in the open, consider investing in a few apothecary jars for holding accessories. Bath salts, soap, and cotton swabs look great in clear glass containers. This way, your guests can help themselves when in the bathroom without having to snoop in your cabinets.

The Bedroom

If you know that your bedroom isn't in a condition that guests would be proud of, you probably will do everything possible to ensure no one spends the night. However, what do you do when you are pushed to the wall whereby you must have guests sleeping over? Obviously, you wouldn't want to be embarrassed by your bedroom because it isn't in a condition that you are proud of. The answer is simple; keep your house clean if you don't want to end up disappointed and embarrassed. Here is how you can go about cleaning the bedroom:

De-cluttering the bedroom

You can bet nobody wants to see his or her sleeping area all that jammed giving you a feeling like you are sleeping in some store down the street. So remember to always keep it spacious by getting rid of anything that does not belong where it is currently. Always make an effort to put away something every time you go to different sections of your house, as this will assist you to get rid of clutter. Remove any clothes lying on the bed by moving them to the laundry area or fold them and put them away in the closet or wardrobe. If you have spoons, plates and cups in the bedroom, place them in the basket to move them where they belong. You can opt to move such items when you are moving towards the kitchen. Every house is different in its layout; some will have a kitchen next to the bedroom while others may have the kitchen far away from the bedrooms. Therefore, ensure that you start from the furthest or closest corner moving to the front or back so it is up to you to choose the strategy that will require minimal movements and time wastage.

Taking care of furniture

We all know you need that dressing table, bedside table, chair, reading desk, bookrack, and whatnot. However, it is best to minimize the number of furniture in your bedroom otherwise; you will simply be adding clutter in there. Your bedroom should be a place for sex, relaxation and sleep so you should really minimize the number of distractions by having minimal furniture. This will also make your cleaning work much easier as you do not have to keep moving too many objects as you clean. Here are some tips to help you de-clutter and organize your bedroom to make it more spacious, airy, and easier to clean.

Have someone else tell you what needs to be moved or removed. You can remove everything out and give room for new suggestions on how to go about the new arrangements. However, remember not to bring back any excess furniture that you may feel is of less importance. Keep in mind that de-cluttering isn't organizing clutter; if you don't need something in the bedroom, keep it out of your bedroom.

Categorize everything into trash, give away, or keep then take the necessary steps to ensure that everything goes where it belongs.

\# Repaint the bedroom using low VOC paint after taking everything out of the bedroom to give the room a fresh and elegant look.

De-clutter your clothing

Piles of clothing, shoes, and other accessories cause setbacks in de-cluttering the bedroom. You don't have to go through your wardrobe to take out anything that doesn't fit you. If you haven't worn anything for the last 6 months or something no longer fits you, give it out or put it in the trash bin. You can as well place two containers in the wardrobe.

Classify the clothes into shirts, trousers, suits, tops and blouses to help you distinguish easily so that you don't have to rummage through your clothes in future to pick out a certain clothing you may be looking for. In addition, you may decide to consider the colors by putting similar colors together. As for the dirty clothes, transfer them to the laundry area for washing.

Cleaning the bedroom surfaces

Wipe all the dust that might have accumulated on doorknobs, bedside tables, and windowsills and if you happen to be having a book cabinet within your bedroom or any other books lying around, remember to dust them clean as well. Any stubborn stains around the bedroom area can be removed by having them wet prior to the removal process. Sweep the floors on your way out after making sure everything is in its rightful position. Spray some air freshener for the final touches.

Bedroom Organization Tips

Clothes are spilling out of your drawers, random items are scattered under the bed and all over the floor, and shoes are littered across the floor. If this sounds familiar, then you may need some organizational tips to keep your space organized.

*Convert side tables into dressers

If you always find your drawers overflowing with clothes, then consider converting your side tables into full dressers for additional storage space.

*Try under-the-bed shelves

Instead of shoving random items haphazardly under your bed, you can utilize your floor space by employing under the bed storage. You can use this spot for storing away exercise gear, extra bed linens, and even handbags.

*Be creative with your furniture

It is not mandatory for your bed to sit against a wall. You can convert tall bookshelves into an eclectic headboard, where you can easily reach your favorite bedtime reads.

*Convert clutter into décor

Extra large frames, random houseplants, old magazines – if these items are cluttering your floor, find a way to arrange them in an artful way that does not make it seem so disorganized. Adding trays and stacking your books can suddenly make a messy corner become a stylish tableau.

*Go for hidden storage

Side tables usually come with small and slim drawers that are barely enough to store your essentials. A better alternative would be a wicker trunk that has enough space for extra blankets and nighttime essentials.

*Store up, and not out

Opt for tall furniture to save space. Swap that wide dresser for a vertical storage that will provide enough space to store extra furniture.

*Divide your drawers

Do not store your jewelry in a random junk drawer. A better storage space would be a classic drawer divider, or even vintage teacups. A cute arrangement will inspire you to keep the organized space neat.

*Get creative with old dimensions

Does your bedroom have strangely shaped corners and unusual angles? You can make the most of your odd room dimensions by investing in furniture that fits. Your bedroom is a sort of puzzle. Do your best to arrange your things in a smart and easy to access way.

*Showcase your favorites

If you have run out of storage space, you can display some of your favorite items to save space. It doesn't matter if you are dealing with unique travel souvenirs or gorgeous clothing –

use your imagination to display your most treasured possessions.

*Make smart furniture decisions

Replace your standard table with one that has extra shelves. It is crucial that you take advantage of any storage space possible, so learn to get creative. Consider viewing your room with fresh eyes, and then ask yourself where you can incorporate more surface area.

*Double up where possible

If you have space for an additional bookcase or dresser, use it. Even if you are not sure what you want to store in the extra piece of furniture, you still need to take advantage of the space. You are more likely to find something you would like to stow away.

The Living Room

De-Clutter The Living Room

The living room gets most of the attention since almost everyone who enters the house has to pass there. You can begin by putting away anything that is considered trash around the house. This will give you a clear start and make it easy to work quickly. Put away items that don't belong in the living room; it could be a pair of socks, dirty cups, dirty utensils and DVDs that are not in their right sleeves. You should have a basket with you so that you can stack everything that needs to be moved to another location. If you have anything in the basket that should be in the living room, place it where it belongs.

If you have kids, get their toys back into cubbies or chests. Comb through each area putting anything that could be out of place into the basket or bin. Unwind any cords that might be twisted then ensure to re-stack magazines, DVDs and CDs and other things that could be scattered all over the entertainment area. Put all remotes in some small box for convenience when needed; they shouldn't be moving from tables to couches, to the carpet and to any other place, you can imagine. Straighten and re-stack any books that need re-arranging.

Telephone

We use the telephone on a daily basis but rarely do we remember to clean it. Hand-held gadgets that are often shared are mostly responsible for the transfer of germs. The cigarette breath, the lotions and the make-up greatly determine how much dirt or germs the telephone can collect. All you need is some rubbing alcohol, disinfectant wipes, cotton swabs and some soft clothing. Start by wiping the phone down with a disinfectant wipe and remove any dirt that may be visible, then go ahead and moisturize the cotton swabs with rubbing alcohol and use them to clean in between the crevices or the outlines of the dial pad and any other region you may find necessary as you proceed. Dry with a soft cloth once done.

Surface cleaning the living room

Use a vacuum cleaner to remove cobwebs from the roof and any dust that may have gathered. Also, clean the couches and seats to remove food particles, dust, and other dirt that may be gathered. Apply a cleaning solution to a wet towel then wipe down the tables, desks, racks, windowsills and blinds. Arrange the cushions properly and pillows to ensure they don't make the living room look messy. Dust baseboards if any and remember to sweep, and damp the floor for ease in cleaning. Vacuum any rugs or carpets in the room and clean any entries to the house where dirt is trapped in easily. Remove any accumulated cobwebs on the walls, the ceiling, and other parts of the living room; you should have gotten rid of these when cleaning other rooms as well. To clean out this, take a long broom-brush, attach a dampened duster at the far end, and run it around the edges of the ceiling. Also, work around the lightings and hanging fixtures to catch any webs dangling from them.

Vacuum or sweep the floor before mopping to remove excess dirt and to make the mopping work much easier. For a fast sweep, move all objects out of the way; this includes placing such items like trashcans, potted plants and other household accessories on higher surfaces or outside the house before starting the cleaning work. As you do that, quickly wipe such items to remove any accumulated dust. Place the mopping equipment in the area where work will begin. Start at the farthest corner and work backwards towards the door. You can use a portable fan at the far end of the room where you have finished mopping to help in fast drying just in case someone may be walking in and out to avoid making the place dirty before it dries.

Organization Tips For The Living Room

Most families use the living room as a gathering area for family members and friends. It is the place where you carry out various activities with the family, and entertain your guests. Living rooms are meant for relaxing, reading, conversations, entertainment, and so on. It is a comfort zone for most people in the family, apart from their own bedrooms. As such, it is very crucial that you make your living room as organized and comfortable as you can. No one likes to live in a cluttered space. A decluttered living room can go a long way towards helping you relieve stress, especially after coming home from a busy workday. You can make your living room more inviting and attractive by organizing everything in it. You won't believe how easy it is to keep your family room organized. You only need discipline and creativity to maintain it. So how can you go about organizing the living room?

*Embrace the wastebasket

If your living room tends to attract all kind of trash, consider including a wastebasket to cut down the clutter. Not many family rooms have a wastebasket, since they are not attractive, and tend to smell. You can counteract this by investing in a can that fits the décor of your room. If food is going to be thrown here, find one with some deodorizing trash bags and a lid.

*Keep flat surfaces clutter free

Magazines, books, papers, and brochures tend to accumulate in flat surfaces all over the house, including the family room. You need to have a household information center, which is highly likely to be the living room. In fact, the living room tends to be more cluttered since it is the central gathering place. The ideal recommendation here is a two drawer lateral file. On average, that is really all the paper you need to run a house. If the floor space is not available, then you can always use a stackable file cart.

Sweep all the flat surfaces quickly, and pile all the papers in a bin, sort them out and then purge as necessary. Ensure you keep papers in files as opposed to over the coffee table.

*Keep out-of-control cords under control

Until the world goes completely wireless, we will always have to deal with tangled cables stuck behind our entertainment centers. The good news is you can do several things to tame the cords in the living room. The slim cable yoyo is the most attractive option. It coils neatly up to 6" of cord, and is designed with an adhesive backing that holds onto almost all surfaces. You can also stick a cable caddy onto your desktop, and this has an added advantage of additional space where you can clamp several cables. However, since the cords will still hang loosely, a cable zipper that encloses all the cables might come in handy.

*Create a play zone

If your kids keep placing toys all over the living room, then it is time to put them under control. You can transform an unused corner of your living room into an excellent play area, since the wall helps prevent encroaching clutter. You can also use an unused corner to place a children's table or a small bookcase. For toy storage, add rolling bins so that your kid does not feel too confined.

*Coffee table functionality

If your living room has a coffee table, you may want to review its organizational capacity. If your coffee table looks great, but doesn't have enough storage space for remote controls, drink coasters, or even magazines, then it's probably making life harder. If you aren't ready to invest in a new one, you can always add low storage cubes, bins or rolling baskets to stick under the table.

*Design a game area

If you are a family that loves to play together, then a game cabinet for cards and board games can be both fun and functional. Most people usually end up stashing games in a television armoire, but it helps to have a separate space for them, whether it is plastic containers beneath the sofa, a bookcase, or a shelving unit. When you create a single game space, you can free up space for storing other items. If you use your computer for gaming, it is generally best not to go for a computer armoire. These rarely work well. A better idea would be to invest in a desk that has a separate surface for the monitor, paper storage and work surface.

*Display photos creatively

If you have plenty of small photo frames that seem to be causing clutter inside your family room, then you may want to take control and display them in different ways. Collage frames and photo albums are great alternatives for storing numerous photos at once, and if you don't use film, a digital photo frame may come in handy. In addition, don't just use the side or mantel tables – make the most of the vertical wall spaces. If you are a scrapbook fan, it may be helpful to organize your photos by date or event in photo boxes, and then place them on a bookshelf in one central location.

*Make the most of the space behind your sofa

Organize excess candles, pillows, and blankets in an accessible area – behind your sofa. This is an ideal place for a low bookcase, cabinet, or trunk. The plus side is that you have an extra space to display some of your treasured objects, or put a lamp.

*Sort out your movie collection

If you are like any other family, you are probably fond of multimedia such as CDs, videotapes and DVDs. Set aside thirty minutes to sort out your entire collection, and place it into to piles: one for donating or selling back, and the other for keeping. If you don't remember the last time you watched the movie, or you no longer listen to that particular music, then you need to let it go. There are several ways you can store your sorted collection: the drawers of a coffee table, ottoman, or in a bookcase; whichever system works for you.

*Grow your houseplants

A green thumb in the family room can be a jungle. Use several decorative pots or a cute plant stand to organize your plants. When looking for a stand, keep in mind that the type of plant you choose to grow will determine its location in the room. Stands usually come in tiered, pedestal or corner configurations, and some are even designed with drawers where you can keep your watering can and fertilizer.

*Keep your collections at bay

If you are not careful with collections, they can take over your living room space, and make it harder to keep it organized. The best way to display large collections is by showing them bits and pieces at a time, and rotating them to keep the décor fresh. Divide your collection into two, put half of the pieces into a proper container, and then store it in a hall closet. You can keep an inventory of individual pieces in the storage bin for additional value, either personal or otherwise.

The Garage

Unknown to many, the garage is the family's meeting point in crucial times. It is the first place where a dad teaches his son how to pop the hood of the car and shows him some basics of a car. It is the same place where that gas smell and oil reminds us of a departed relation. Therefore, it is good to go in and do some thorough cleaning regularly.

De-Cluttering The Garage

You should not leave tools lying around on the garage floor. Have them shelved and if you do not have a shelf ready, then you should consider buying or constructing one. This will ensure that there are no accidents around the garage area. Have plastic containers and bins to keep in the different tools and spare parts. Make sure that the bins fit on the shelves before buying. These containers can be categorized as trash, sale/donation, action items that need to be looked at, and loose parts and tools. Another categorization can be grouping items into tools, sports gear, equipment, garden and lawn equipment, seasonal or lawn furniture, bolts and nuts, and other small parts.

The garage in most cases is used for dumping stuff like broken cookers, freezers, and even toys. Look for the services of a dumping company to dump such huge equipment and you can as well give them out for charity to avoid cluttering your garage.

Below is an effective way of how you can de-clutter and organize.

*Assess, analyze, & prioritize

One of the most common problems most people encounter when organizing the garage is lack of a plan for the space. It is important to take the time to scrutinize and visualize the space to determine what you want to use it for. What is your priority for the garage? Do you want to use it for storing sporting equipment and seasonal items, as a workspace, or to park your car? Or perhaps, all the above? If you take the time to plan for your garage, you may be able to incorporate all these functions. Putting your priorities in line will make it easier to purge and organize the space, since you will be able to determine what you want to go into the space, and what you don't want.

*Clear and clean the space

Starting with a clean space is the only effective approach. Find a few blankets and tarps, and then align them in an open area like a lawn or driveway to place your items. Once you have removed everything, clean the space as well as the floors.

You can ask for some assistance to help in cleaning the garage as it may involve moving some heavy equipment. Just take a vacuum and suck all that trash before embarking on some serious cleaning. Well, unlike other rooms, the garage does not need a mop to clean its floors. Just evaluate everything that may be remaining in the garage after you removed some items out and be sure that nothing stands to be damaged because all you have to do is flood the floor using a hosepipe. Take the nozzle, aim at the floors and even walls if necessary, and drive out the dirt with water. When you are almost done, you can sweep excess water using a hard broom and you will be surprised at how easy the work would have been made. If you trust your neighborhood, you can leave all the garage doors open overnight so that by morning, the water will have dried.

You may also want to use this chance to stain your concrete floor and paint the walls, in order to give your garage a new, fresh, clean look.

*Sort like items together

When pulling things out of your garage, sort all your sporting equipment in one spot, your decorations in another spot, then your camping gear, lawn gear, and so on. The screws and nails can also be put together in one spot.

*Start purging

This is not the time to be sentimental about the items you have stored in your garage. You need to be ruthless here. Try to get rid of as much as fifty percent of the items in your space. You don't necessarily have to lose that much, but making the effort will go a long way. Start by establishing four piles for recycling, trashing, donating, and keeping. As you continue purging, place every item into its relevant category. If there is anything you haven't used for more than one year, get rid of it along with the broken items.

Return anything that does not belong in the garage or that is not yours, and eliminate duplicates. Keep in mind that the point is to organize your garage. How many rakes, bats, basketballs, brooms, screws, and hammers do you actually need? If you are finding it hard to get rid of stuff, ask yourself these questions: do you use it? Do you love it? Have you used it in the last one year? Do you really need it? Anything whose answers are in the negative should go to the recycle, donate or trash pile.

*Take inventory of your items

Now that you have trimmed everything down to what you actually need, the next point is to take inventory of what is left. This will give you a good idea of what organizational items you will need to purchase, and what you can work with. As a general rule of thumb, avoid purchasing organizational tools before you have purged. It will save you money, time, and lots of frustration. Next, map out the space. Use masking tape to mark out different work zones/spaces, or draw it out on paper. You can mark off the spot you have reserved for heavy-duty shelving, your car, paint & hazardous material cabinet, lawn care supplies, sports equipment, workbench or tools shed, and recreational equipment. Remember to go overhead and vertical. You can also hang items on your walls, or install shelving.

And the ceiling? You can install plywood boards under rafters to keep seldom-used items or seasonal things. In addition, it is important to consider frequency of use and convenience. For instance, it is a good idea to have a trashcan close to the driver's side door of your car, where you can throw away items easily. You can also place recycling bins at the door leading to the house so that you can toss items easily. Bikes can also occupy the space near the garage door so that the kids can easily grab their bikes when needed.

*Determine your organizational supplies

Once you have finished mapping out your zones, it is time to gather your supplies. Find large trashcans to store brooms, shovels, and rakes upright. Sporting equipment such as gloves, bats, balls, and skateboards can also be stored using large trashcans. Hang tools using pegboards. Use large hooks attached to the ceiling or the wall to hang extension cords and bicycles. Get a cabinet with locking doors to store your chemicals, paint, cleaning supplies, and such other hazardous materials. Use metal or solid wood shelves to store storage bins and heavy equipment. Store like items using clear plastic containers.

Consider investing in a rolling tool rack or cabinet to keep supplies organized while transporting them. Use small plastic containers or glass jars to keep washers, hooks, nuts, screws, and nails organized. Store screwdrivers, and paint brushes in tin cans.

Place a doormat at the entrance to the house to dust off shoes before entering. Lastly, find a label marker. Labeling things will help you organize your items like never before.

*Put everything in its rightful zone

This is the best part, where you can actually see the finishing line. Start storing everything in its designated spot, and start labeling. Label makers are a very efficient tool. They make it easier to find items, and put them away. You can use label makers to label your shelves, boxes, drawers, containers, and cords. If you do not have a label maker, you can always use a permanent marker and duct tape or masking tape. Ensure that you have labeled the sides and front of your storage bins so that you can be able to read them from any way that you place them. As far as labeling is concerned, the ideas are endless. The main thing to note is to label as many things as you can.

Cleaning Other Parts Of The House

The Corridors

After cleaning the living room, you can head to the corridors on your way out or when moving to another room; the layout of your house will determine where you are headed to. As you move, sweep the floors and then finish off by mopping using a damp cloth or a mop.

Box and stoppage

If you are having problems with throwing away some stuff you consider important in some way although you rarely use them or you may even never get to put them into use, just stuff them in boxes and label the boxes with a word like 'clutter' or something. After labeling, you can put the boxes away somewhere like the garage or the attic. If you don't need anything that is in the box for over 6 months, donate everything that is in there to charity without even opening the box.

Tips for boxing items

If you are at crossroads on whether to giveaway or retain something, follow these simple questions:

#Do you like it.

#Do you often use it?

#Do you really need it now or in the long run?

Once you come up with answers to the above questions, weigh the positive against the negatives and make a quick decision without wasting any time. Drop it into the trashcan if it amounts to trash or keep it in your archived items and save yourself the headache of giving it a second thought as you embark on the rest of the house-cleaning chore.

Windows

It is always advisable to keep the windows wide open whenever possible to allow fresh air into the house. Stuffiness and lack of fresh air can be a trigger for respiratory problems especially if you are living in a house that is not well ventilated.

How To Clean Windows Well

It is wrong to use wadded up paper towels or newspapers, spray cleaner or elbow grease as these items will end up making the panes look dirtier by spreading the stains. It won't matter how much you will keep rubbing but in reality all you will be doing is moving dirt from one spot to another and that will not be of much help. When you are done, the window will keep looking dirty or even worse. You may then be wondering how you can actually do the cleaning work perfectly well. As you start the process, it is important to note that the windows should be best cleaned on a cloudy day since cleaning them on a sunny warm day will make the washing solution dry out quickly and cause streaking, giving it a bad finish. So how do you do proper cleaning during the cloudy day?

Tools

Most people prefer to use Squeegee, a T-Shaped cleaning tool, with a flat rubber blade that is best suited to remove all the dirt from the windowpanes. If you can't find Squeegee, you can opt for a sponge and towel to dry when you are done. The good thing about a squeegee is that it cleans in one single swoop hence no need of using a towel again to do the drying. It is preferred because it makes the job to be done much faster.

Below is a list of the right tools that can help you get the work done:

#A sponge

#A squeegee

#Light bristled brush

#Clean lint-free cloths

#Paper towels

#A sponge mop

#A Soft scrub

Choose your best window cleaning solution and apply it to the window using the Squeegee or the sponge. Soap and water is another good window cleaning solution you may require here. It is good for cleaning the interior side of the windows because the inside part of a window is not usually as dirty as the exterior. Just mix a gallon of warm water and a teaspoon of dishwashing soap in a bucket.

Ammonia and Vinegar is also another solution that can be used. Mix 8 cups of warm water, two cups of rubbing alcohol and half cup of ammonia with one tablespoon hand dishwashing detergent in a bucket.

Interior window

Using a vacuum cleaner, vacuum the windowsills and tracks to get rid of dirt and any other debris that could be trapped on them. You can use a Q-tip or any other applicable tool to remove any build-up of gunk in the corners. Vacuum the window tracks and windowsills to remove dirt and debris.

Exterior window

For the exterior windows, remove any window screens and mark them if you can so that you will know which window goes to where when you are done. Pre-rinse before washing to ensure no scratches while you are cleaning.

It is advisable to clean your windows very regularly to make them look great always and to allow natural light to penetrate into different parts of the house.

The Laundry room

Once every other place in the house is sparkling clean, you should probably have many dusty or dirty clothes that you have collected from different parts of your home. So, the next and final step should be to clean all clothes in the laundry area and then clean the washing machine. Start by de-cluttering the room or area by removing anything that shouldn't be in the laundry room including trash then move on to clean the ceiling, the walls and the floor using cleaning solution. Clean all the shoes and clothes using the manufacturer's recommended cleaning approach then place them somewhere they can get fresh air before you can fold them and distribute them to the respective rooms.

Washing machine

It is very common to find the washing machine being ignored despite the fact that it is used to do a cleaning job itself. In cleaning the washing machine, fill it with hot water and add a cup of detergent then run a complete cycle with just hot water to clean. Run another round with hot water to rinse. Also cleaning the inside with vinegar will help get rid of soap build up and lingering mildew. Finally fill warm water and run one cycle to rinse the machine.

Conclusion

Every house is different; the layout of your house will largely determine the approach that you should take when cleaning different rooms. Additionally, the number of rooms in your house will probably be different from what I have discussed in this book.

It is important to use the information you have gathered in this book and modify it to fit your cleaning needs and goals. Obviously, your speed will be dependent on the size of your house, your cleaning speed, the amount of accumulated dirt and clutter in the house and a host of other factors. So, while someone may take 20 minutes to de-clutter and clean his or her bedroom, someone else may need 40 minutes to get this done. All in all, use the least movements when cleaning and ensure that every movement counts in making your house clean and clutter free.

If you would like to subscribe to receive free e-books on Kindle when they are available, just Click on this Link

Finally, if you enjoyed this book, please take the time to share your thoughts and post a review on Amazon. It will be greatly appreciated!

Thank you and good luck!

monetary loss due to the information herein, either directly or indirectly.

Respective authors own all copyrights not held by the publisher.

The information herein is offered for informational purposes solely, and is universal as so. The presentation of the information is without contract or any type of guarantee assurance.

The trademarks that are used are without any consent, and the publication of the trademark is without permission or backing by the trademark owner. All trademarks and brands within this book are for clarifying purposes only and are the owned by the owners themselves, not affiliated with this document.

Printed in Great Britain
by Amazon

62244852R00031